The route of the Exodus superimposed on an aerial photograph taken from a satellite. Th solid line represents the conventionally-accepted route. The dotted line shows the rout suggested by modern scholars.

AN ISRAEL HAGGADAH

הַגָּדָה שֶׁל פֶּסַח

An ISRAEL

HAGGADAH

FOR PASSOVER

adapted by Meyer Levin

HARRY N. ABRAMS, INC.

PUBLISHERS

The painting reproduced on pages 108–9 was created especially for this book by Reuven Rubin

Twelfth printing, 1993

ISBN 0–8109–2040–9
Library of Congress Catalog Card Number: 70–99933

Published by Harry N. Abrams, Incorporated, New York
A Times Mirror Company

Printed and bound in Japan

CONTENTS

AN ISRAEL HAGGADAH

PREFACE

This Haggadah is presented not in disagreement with tradition but to restore to our Passover observance something of its earlier tradition of spontaneity, of connection to current life, and hence to universal freedom efforts. It is called an "Israel" Haggadah because such a renewed and enlivened tradition has already come into being in Israel, particularly in the kibbutz movement where a variety of texts is in use.

In Israel, the Exodus from Egypt is an ever-present reality because of direct, continuous contact with historic sites, and we have therefore tried to convey that contact through photographs. Finally, in Israel the Passover is celebrated in many variations, and yet in unity, by Jews from all over the world—by Algerians, Americans, Australians, Bokharans, Europeans, Yemenites, from the ultra-orthodox to the atheistic. *An Israel Haggadah*, then, aspires to bring to the celebrant a sense of participation in this unity.

The aim in this Haggadah has been to include the beautiful and unforgettable utterances of tradition in an adaptation that will make the Seder more pertinent to many who had come to regard it as rote, and to others who had altogether abandoned, or had never undertaken, the Passover observance.

Haggadah means "what is said." Seder means the order of events, or, if one wishes, the program. The Passover Haggadah is what is said, sung, recited, and enacted each year at the family feast called the Seder, a joyous celebration and something of a rite, but not a sacerdotal ritual, held in remembrance of the Exodus from slavery in Egypt.

But Haggadah in a broader sense means legendry, the telling of tales. In Jewish lore it means the shimmering cloak of myth and parable woven around Biblical Law. Thus the Passover Seder is not an act of cultish worship, but a free recital around several traditionally obligatory points, some of which recall the priestly services at the Temple.

The Seder begins with an open call of the most resounding universality, "Let all who are hungered, come and eat!" A child asks Four Questions, about just those things a child would notice—a different way of sitting, and an odd assortment of foods. The answers tell him the meaning of slavery and freedom. Then everyone at the table makes an astounding avowal—each person present must regard himself as though he, personally, was brought forth from slavery!

After this come various psalms, wisdom-sayings, symbolic displays, tastings of symbolic foods, then songs, riddles, pledges. The Haggadah itself informs us there is great latitude in the service, for it quotes an early sage, Rabbi Gamaliel, who cautioned that whoever does not deal with the meaning of these three things, pesach (the Passover lamb), matzah, and maror (the bitter herb), has not truly celebrated this festival.

Certain avowals and blessings in the Seder are hallowed; the words pierce us like the call of the shofar. But much of the explanation in the Haggadah may be given in one's own words, and the texts offered here need not be strictly adhered to. For the Seder is a personal enactment. It is at one and the same time a play for young children, with songs and games to keep them awake, a teach-in, a solemn religious occasion, an archaic rite of spring, a wine-bibbing, a dedication. The Seder harmoniously puts together such wondrously diverse elements as exalted hymns, nursery rhymes, historical recitations, a treasure hunt (for the hidden half of the ritual matzah), an apparition (Elijah's visit), a feat of magic (the emptying of Elijah's wine cup), and a philosophical ditty, Chad Gadya.

The ceremony is what we would today call child-oriented, following the Passover instruction in Exodus (13:8): *And thou shalt tell thy son in that day,* and again (12:26, 27): *And it shall come to pass, when your children shall say unto you: What mean ye by this service? that ye shall say: It is the sacrifice of the Lord's passover, for that He passed over the houses of the children of Israel in Egypt, when He smote the Egyptians, ...*

But the original, mysterious word for Passover, *pesach*, also refers to the sacrificial lamb, in some archaic rite of spring that preceded the Exodus, the bondage in Egypt, perhaps even preceded the time of Abraham, in the cultish spring festivals of primitive man. Early Zionist settlers, in their determined effort to create a new Jewish return to the soil, harked back to the agricultural nature of the feast, introducing sheep-shearing festivals, and reviving the ceremony of the cutting of the first grain, the omer, accompanied by dancing in the fields.

Sheep shearing in Emek Israel

In the time of the Temples, this rite of spring was combined with the Passover celebration of the Exodus from Egypt. Devout Jews from all over the country made the pilgrimage to the Holy Place in Jerusalem for the freedom festival, each bringing his sheep into the Temple courtyard and awaiting his turn in the throng, as the priests, intoning psalms in praise of the Lord, performed the sacrifice. The sanctified meat was roasted that night for the family Seder, when the freedom tale was retold.

Bringing in the sheaves at Ben Shemen, a youth center

Cutting of the first grain, called the omer, in Kibbutz Revivim

Field celebration of the Counting of the Omer in Yokneam

With the destruction of the Second Temple by the Romans in 70 C.E., there was no Holy Place, and the offerings could no longer be sanctified. And so the Jews from then on, wherever they found themselves, conducted their Pesach without the central object, the sanctified lamb. Only a symbol of the sacrifice was displayed at the feast: the shank bone. Also symbolizing or replacing the lamb, some say, is the ceremonial matzah, the middle one of the three that are placed at the head of the table. This matzah is broken in half, with one part hidden, to be found and brought back by the children at the end of the meal, when it is shared and eaten—some say as dessert, some say in place of the lamb. Others say the hiding is a device to keep the children awake and alert throughout the Seder. This custom, incidentally, is not found in early Haggadoth of the Middle East Jewish communities.

Probably the closest approximation of a Passover ceremony in Biblical times is the Seder held each year by the Samaritans on the stony top of Mount Gerizim, which this sect has always considered, in opposition to Jerusalem, as the Holy Place. Now numbering scarcely two hundred souls, the Samaritans claim unbroken descent from the family of the High Priest Aaron, but because of an ancient schism, they were not admitted as Jews by the Temple authorities.

For their Seder, the Samaritan families assemble on their mountaintop. Selected sheep are sacrificed by the sacerdotal leaders, and then baked in a covered pit. The pit is opened to the chanting of psalms, and each family then holds its feast, eating the offering on pieces of matzah while standing, in literal re-enactment of the hasty departure and flight from Egypt.

But the Seder has developed rather differently in the congregations of Israel in the Diaspora. Suggestions for the ceremony, including questions such as are asked by the youngest child at each Seder today, were already included in the Mishnah, the part of the Talmud compiled in the second century. The awesome Psalm CXIII, and the wildly jubilant Psalm CXIV, sung by the Temple priests, were now chanted at the meal. Gradually, over the centuries, in Jewish communities dispersed in many lands, various sayings and songs and commentaries on commentaries were added.

Since not every family head thought himself capable of remembering "what is said," the Seder began to be written out. The oldest Haggadah as yet discovered is a parchment from before the eighth century C.E., found in an ancient Cairo synagogue, in the genizah, or repository for worn-out scriptures. In basic form, including the drinking of the four cups of wine, the observance is like today's. But the opening of the door for Elijah, and some of the involved commentaries, were interjected later. By the Middle Ages the Haggadah was what it is now, with variations in different lands.

Before and even after the advent of printing, the Haggadah was copied out by hand and often beautifully illuminated, as in the noted fourteenth-century manuscript preserved in Sarajevo. Among the first books to be printed were Haggadoth, and various woodcut and later copperplate editions from Prague, Venice, and Amsterdam, are highly prized. In modern times, at least two elaborately illustrated editions have a wide circulation, those by Arthur Szyk, and Ben Shahn. But while it is most gratifying to have a beautiful Haggadah for show, there remains

Passover of the Samaritans on Mount Gerizim

the question of the Haggadah for use. This Haggadah is designed for use; therefore, its rearrangement of some parts of the text, so as to recover their meaningfulness. We trust, however, that our Haggadah will also be found beautiful.

According to the historian Cecil Roth, more than twenty-seven hundred editions of the Passover Haggadah have appeared in various languages. Few of them depart from the "established" text. A Reform version was offered in Germany by Leopold Stein in 1841, and this was adapted in America, in the Union Prayer Book of 1892. The current revision, published by the Central Conference of American Rabbis, is dated 1923. It is brief and more readily followed than the Orthodox version. The Reconstructionist *New Haggadah*, first issued in 1941, stresses the social relevance and universality of Passover. Maurice Samuel has published his version of the Haggadah, and revisions by individual rabbis are numerous. There is even a "radical" Seder offered by the New Left, with special pleadings on current political issues.

And yet our most commonly available Haggadah, often handed out with packaged Passover products, contains a text with so many accretions, such clumsy English locutions, and such complex directions, as to discourage many from holding the Passover. Children, for whom the occasion is intended, become bored. If there is an elder present who "knows how" to conduct the Seder in "the old way," he often drones out the words in Hebrew, unfortunately understood by few. (He himself may know only how to read the sounds by alphabet, without understanding the words.) He skips, and jumps back and forth to different pages. People give up trying to follow, they are getting hungry, the recital turns into a rapid gibberish, bringing a general sigh of relief when it is finally announced that eating can begin. The freedom festival itself has become slavishly imprisoned in rigid form.

Curiously, this view of the Seder as an untouchable ritual may be seen, psychologically, as perhaps a result of the link between the Passover Seder and a Christian rite. Almost everyone knows that the Last Supper was a Seder, and most Jews vaguely understand that the Catholic communion, using the wafer and the wine, transforms elements of the Passover—the matzah and the wine. By reversal, this gives Jews the impression that just as a Catholic communion is a fixed ritual, so too must be the Seder!

In the Middle Ages, Christians confusedly connected their own beliefs about wine and blood with their conviction that the Jewish Seder was a mysterious sacerdotal rite—and thus arose their wild accusations that in the making of the matzah, the blood of a Christian child was mixed in.

Up to the present century, in the notorious Beilis trial in Kiev in 1912, the "blood accusation" kept recurring, and one hears echoes of it even now. It might have been in the hope of disproving such horror stories that the custom of opening the door for Elijah was adopted, to show the innocence of the feast.

In America, the sense of rigidity in the service, and of strictly orthodox observances that were increasingly distant from the ways of many modern, less attached Jews, led to widespread abandonment of the Seder. This process of estrangement is reflected in Seder scenes in American Jewish novels, such as *Marjorie Morningstar* by Herman Wouk, in which a sophisticated young Jew walks out before the festival is over, and in my own *The Old Bunch,* where a non-Jew is entertained by a young couple who show their emancipation by serving ham!

More recently there has been a renewal of interest in the Seder, partly out of nostalgia, and partly, it must be admitted, through campaigns saturated with advertising for prepared Passover foods. The time has come to restore the relevance of this most meaningful service.

Some years ago I asked a good friend of mine, a liberal, intelligent young family man, what he was doing for Passover. "We used to have a big family Seder with my parents," he said, "but since my father died, and I really can't follow those complicated instructions in the Haggadah, we just have a big meal."

I took a fresh look at the Haggadah. A child asks the Four Questions. Is he answered? All sorts of dissertations intervene, so that when the answers do come, they can scarcely be connected with the questions. And by then the child is probably half-asleep. A Biblical narration begins, with the story of Abraham, but becomes entangled in rabbinical word-play. And the English! While the archaic locutions offered for the American generation have a certain charm, the effect is of ritualistic incantation rather than of clear meaning. No wonder observance declined. Yet at the same time I found observance being revitalized in Palestine, particularly in the "unreligious" kibbutzim.

While many of the early settlers were rather hostile to formal religious worship, an urge to celebrate the Passover with something more than a field ceremony remained. The Counting of the Omer would be followed by a group Seder, using a new Haggadah with avowals expressing the ideals of the kibbutz, and with modern variations of the Four Questions, on social issues, recited by the children in chorus. The kibbutz Seder became a favorite with visitors, who might find themselves at the same table with a cabinet member or a premier, for many members of the government, when Israel attained nationhood, were old-time kibbutzniks who always went back home for Passover, and others—like Golda Meir—had grown children in the kibbutzim.

The Four Questions at Kibbutz Yotfata

Over the years, I saw the kibbutz Seder returning somewhat toward the traditional. In Meshek Yagur, where I repeatedly visited, the composer Yehuda Sharett—my roommate in 1929—eventually created a complete Seder setting, with choral music, orchestra, and recitations from amongst the members. Yagur is now one of the largest kibbutzim, and in its vast hall over fifteen hundred people partake each year in this inspired ceremony.

It was this free-spirited blending of the traditional with the modern that led me to attempt to revise the family Haggadah in a way that I felt would be more meaningful to my own generation, while retaining all that I felt beautiful and perfect in the "old country" Haggadah. I have also kept those elements that by consensus are the essence of the ceremony and should not be altered.

What I have attempted is somewhat in the nature of a dramatic adaptation. I have tried to restore the Seder as a family enactment, in a text that is simple to follow, not overlong, basically traditional, but also bringing the vastly significant events of recent Jewish experience into the timelessness of the Passover.

From year to year I have used this Haggadah, changing and adapting it, until it settled into its present form. Increasingly, guests have asked for copies for their own future use. The text was first published by Behrman House in 1968, and I am indebted to Jacob Behrman and to Rabbi David Passow for suggestions which I have incorporated into this version, as well as to Harry Coopersmith for the arrangement of traditional songs.

One year, in New York, we conducted our Seder with several Negro friends, whose participation brought out the profound universal nature of this freedom affirmation. Another year, we used this Haggadah in an open-air Seder on Herzlia beach, below our home in Israel. Among our guests were two Arab couples. A roasted sheep was the center of the feast.

While I have eliminated certain pilpulistic discussions that were perhaps fascinating to the Talmud-trained Jewry of other days, such as whether a day means a day and a night or only a day, I have introduced certain explanations for today's less traditional Jews that clarify various customs, such as the visit of Elijah.

After the recital of the Ten Plagues, I have inserted a recital of the Ten Commandments. I have, as far as possible, carried the narrative itself back to the Biblical narrative. I have included two of the most

Making pittah

Baking matzoth

inspiring utterances on social justice, from the Prophets. And I have added a memorial for the martyrs of the Holocaust and the heroes of the European ghettos and of Israel.

Some years ago I attended a Seder at the home of the Chief Rabbi of Istanbul. In the traditional way, verses of the narration were chanted in turn around the table. Though few in our time learn this cantilation, I have tried to keep the feeling of participation throughout this Haggadah, by constant changes in who is speaking.

Last Passover we were guests at the home of David Passow, in Brooklyn. There were sons and daughters of college and high-school age. We started off on this Haggadah, and somewhere in the middle the young people veered onto a discussion of campus revolts, Negro rights, Vietnam, and hunger all over the world. Suddenly we realized it had become very late. Thus, we had been behaving in the tradition of the sages of ancient times in B'nai B'rak, whose tale became included in the Haggadah itself, because they were so involved in a discussion of the meaning of the escape from bondage that dawn arrived before they had completed their Seder.

And that's how a Seder should be.

Have a joyous feast! *Chag Sameyach!*

MEYER LEVIN

INTRODUCTION

THE PREPARATION

In a household where Orthodox rules are followed, the separation of Passover from the rest of the year is even more notable than the separation of Sabbath from the rest of the week. For Passover, the entire household is purified. The dwelling is truly made "kosher for Pesach."

Such a household will usually possess a totally separate supply of Passover dishware and utensils, and not one of these articles may come into contact with anything used during the rest of the year. The Passover dishes will be brought out after the non-Passover plates are stored away for the duration of the holiday. If the family does not possess separate dishware, pots, and utensils for Passover, an established ritual of purification involving boiling water, and burial in the ground, must be followed.

Burning the chametz

A matzoth-bringer in Jerusalem

Matzoth cover from Poland, 1908 (Israel Museum, Jerusalem)

As the dominant symbol of Passover is the eating of the "bread of affliction," or flat matzoth, during the entire holiday, the preparation of the matzoth in Orthodox communities extends back to watching the fields in which the grain is grown, to make sure that none of it becomes fermented through rotting. The flat cakes of the Exodus were hastily made from dough that was not set aside to ferment and rise—and one may indeed see the Bedouin of the Sinai today making the same flat bread, or pittah, from a dough of flour and water that is at once baked over a small fire.

In medieval times matzah was baked at home, and later, in communal ovens. The lines of perforations, to keep the matzah from rising during the baking, were made with a wheel with pointed teeth, called a reidel. Now, matzah is factory-made under rabbinical supervision.

A final ceremony is the search for leftover chametz, or leavened bread, that takes place in each Orthodox home on the night before the Seder. This is done in a family procession, led by the father holding a candle. A few crumbs, purposely left by the wife after an intensive Passover housecleaning, are carefully swept up with a feather into a wooden scoop, and taken out to be burned, feather, scoop, and all.

In the modern, less observant household, the meaning of Passover is celebrated without strict obedience to rules and taboos. "Kosher for Passover" is stamped on numerous packaged products. However, the ceremonial items still must be assembled and prepared.

First, the ceremonial matzoth. These are three matzoth, once the special matzoth of watched fields, now ordinary samples. They are placed at the head of the table, and covered. They may be under a napkin, or inside a special matzah cover, which is usually embroidered.

Then, there is the Passover plate, on which the five symbolic foods are displayed. An ordinary large plate may be used, but ceremonial platters, in silver, or porcelain, of ancient or modern design, with sections for each food, enhance the Seder table.

The foods to be presented are as follows:

1. *Spring greens.* Celery, lettuce, or sprigs of parsley may be used. There should be enough so that each person may be handed a small portion for "dipping" during the service.
2. *A roasted egg.* This is to be held aloft for display.
3. *A roasted shank bone of lamb.* This bone is meatless, and is also for display, symbolizing the sacrificial lamb of ancient times.

Majolica Passover plate from Padua, 1673 (Israel Museum, Jerusalem)

4. *The bitter herb.* A horseradish is displayed on the ceremonial plate, but as portions of the bitter herb are eaten during the ceremony, it is best to provide servers within reach of everyone at the table. Wafer-thin slices of horseradish are more practical than ground horseradish.
5. *Charoset.* This unique Passover dish is a spread made out of finely chopped apples, almonds, and raisins, seasoned with cinnamon and made into a paste with sweet wine. Again, a small portion is displayed on the Passover plate, while more is within reach for everyone at the table. In color and consistency, charoset resembles mortar.

In addition to these five items on the ceremonial platter, a dish of salt water is provided for the dipping of the greens. If the group is small, the leader of the Seder may dip each portion of the greens as he hands it out, but if many people are present, it is best to have a salt water dish within reach of each person. A widely observed custom is to provide a hard-boiled egg in a dish of salt water at each setting. This may be eaten as an appetizer.

Finally, there are provisions of matzoth, and flasks of wine, enough to provide four cups for each person. Various confections and little gifts may be hidden around the room for the children's hunt that comes toward the end of the feast.

The Seder meal itself, in Biblical times, consisted of roast lamb, but today dishes vary all over the world. In the tradition of East European Jewry, the feast usually begins with gefüllte fish, followed by chicken soup with matzah balls. Honey cake, and sponge cake with tea, are customary at Passover. After the meal one should linger, cracking walnuts, eating fruit and macaroons, candies, and Passover honey dips called teiglach.

THE PASSOVER TABLE

To set the table for this most meaningful of holiday feasts, the best that the household has to offer is put to use. On the glistening white tablecloth the polished candlesticks are centered, with the candles ready for the blessing and lighting. Flowers and blossoms provide a springtime air. Plates piled with matzoth, wine-filled decanters, bowls of fruit, dishes of confections, nuts, and raisins give the table an additional festive allure. Beside each setting is a Haggadah.

Prominently placed toward the head of the table is the wine goblet for Elijah. Facing the leader of the Seder is the ceremonial Passover plate, with its five symbolic foods: the greens, a roasted egg, a shank bone of lamb, the horseradish, and the charoset.

To the right of the Passover plate lie the three covered matzoth. The meaning of each will be explained during the Seder.

Thus the Passover table is set.

The chair at the head of the table is usually an armchair, provided with pillows, to demonstrate the custom of reclining at ease, like a Roman freeman, during the meal. All who take part in the Seder may use pillows as well.

It is customarily the head of the family who conducts the Seder, calling upon others to read, sing, or recite in turn or in unison. But sometimes an elder guest or a distinguished visitor may be asked to lead the observance. Large group Seders have become common, sometimes as second or even third Seders on succeeding nights, held by various organizations. But community Seders for the first night, and vacation hotel Seders are also becoming popular. In this Haggadah, to remind us of the original, family nature of the feast, the leader of the Seder is designated as Father. Similarly, though the blessing of the candles, and specified womanly readings such as the selection from the Song of Songs, may be performed by mother, daughter, or woman guest, as called upon, the designation here is Mother.

The traditional blessings and avowals that should be recited in Hebrew are printed with transliteration. An English translation is included and may be recited as well. The songs are printed with transliteration of the Hebrew, but the English words printed below will also fit the music. And, of course, other appropriate favorite songs may be freely added, on and on into the night. . . .

THE SEDER

[The words enclosed in brackets are added when the Seder is celebrated on a Friday evening.]

All have taken their places.
The first cup of wine is filled.
Mother lights the candles.

MOTHER

בָּרוּךְ אַתָּה יְיָ, אֱלֹהֵינוּ מֶלֶךְ הָעוֹלָם, אֲשֶׁר קִדְּשָׁנוּ
בְּמִצְוֹתָיו, וְצִוָּנוּ לְהַדְלִיק נֵר שֶׁל [שַׁבָּת וְ]יוֹם טוֹב.

Baruch Atah Adonai, Elohaynu Melech ha-olam, asher kid'shanu b'mitzvotav, v'tzivahnu l'hadlik nayr shel [Shabbath v'] Yom Tov.

Blessed art Thou, Eternal our God, King of the universe, who hast sanctified us through Thy commandments and instructed us to kindle the *[Sabbath and]* holiday candles.

Father: Together with our fellow Jews everywhere, we celebrate tonight the eternal story of the Jewish people, forever linked with man's divine passion for justice and human liberty.

In this, our great yearly feast of liberation, we give thanks to the Eternal for the preservation of our spirit through every brutality, through both defeat and victory. We give thanks for the event that became the great symbol of liberation, the Exodus from Egypt. We give thanks for the divine inspiration that taught us to live by law. We give thanks for the first laws proclaiming the dignity of man: the Ten Commandments, the Torah, and the Sabbath of rest for all—a hallowed day of contemplation when servant and master are reminded that in God's law all are equal.

Father raises his wineglass.

We shall drink the first of the four cups of the Passover Seder—to liberation. We begin with the holiday sanctification, the Kiddush.

בָּרוּךְ אַתָּה יְיָ, אֱלֹהֵינוּ מֶלֶךְ הָעוֹלָם, אֲשֶׁר בָּחַר־
בָּנוּ מִכָּל־עָם וְרוֹמְמָנוּ מִכָּל־לָשׁוֹן וְקִדְּשָׁנוּ
בְּמִצְוֹתָיו. וַתִּתֶּן־לָנוּ יְיָ אֱלֹהֵינוּ בְּאַהֲבָה [שַׁבָּתוֹת
לִמְנוּחָה וּ]מוֹעֲדִים לְשִׂמְחָה חַגִּים וּזְמַנִּים לְשָׂשׂוֹן אֶת־
יוֹם חַג הַמַּצּוֹת הַזֶּה. זְמַן חֵרוּתֵנוּ [בְּאַהֲבָה] מִקְרָא
קֹדֶשׁ זֵכֶר לִיצִיאַת מִצְרָיִם. כִּי בָנוּ בָחַרְתָּ וְאוֹתָנוּ
קִדַּשְׁתָּ מִכָּל־הָעַמִּים [וְשַׁבָּת וּ]מוֹעֲדֵי קָדְשְׁךָ בְּאַהֲבָה
וּבְרָצוֹן בְּשִׂמְחָה וּבְשָׂשׂוֹן הִנְחַלְתָּנוּ. בָּרוּךְ אַתָּה יְיָ
מְקַדֵּשׁ [הַשַּׁבָּת וְ]יִשְׂרָאֵל וְהַזְּמַנִּים:

Baruch Atah Adonai, Elohaynu Melech ha-olam, asher bachaar-baanu mi-kol ahm v'romamanu mi-kol lashon v'kidshanu b'mitzvotav. Vatiten-lanu Adonai Elohaynu b'ahava [Shabbatot limnoochah oo-] moadim l'simcha chaagim oo-zmanim l'saason et yom chag ha-matzoth hazeh. Zman chayrutaynu [b'ahava] mikraa kodesh zaycher litziath Mitzrayim Kih vanu bachartah v'otahnu kidashta mikol ha-amim [v'Shabbath oo-] moaday kodsh'cha b'ahava oo-v'rahtson b'simcha oo-v'saason hinchaltanu. Baruch Atah Adonai m'kadesh [ha Shabbath v'] Yisrael v'hazmanim.

Blessed art Thou, Eternal our God, King of the universe, who selected us from among all people, and exalted us among all tongues, and hallowed us with Thy commandments. Lovingly Thou hast given us, Lord our God, times for joy, seasons for celebration, and this feast of Matzah for the anniversary of our becoming free—a sacred occasion, a remembrance [with love,] of our release from Egypt. For us didst Thou select, and ourselves didst Thou hallow among all peoples. It has been Thy loving will to bestow on us [the Sabbath and] Thy sanctified holidays, for joy and gladness. Blessed art Thou, Lord, who sanctifies [the Sabbath,] Israel, and the holidays.

Before each of the four cups, we shall say the blessing for wine.

All raise their wine cups.

Golden Kiddush cup from Nuremberg, Germany, 1765 (Israel Museum, Jerusalem)

ALL

Grape motif from the ancient synagogue at Chorazin

בָּרוּךְ אַתָּה יְיָ, אֱלֹהֵינוּ מֶלֶךְ הָעוֹלָם, בּוֹרֵא פְּרִי הַגָּפֶן.

Baruch Atah Adonai, Elohaynu Melech ha-olam, boray p'ri ha-gafen.

Blessed art Thou, Eternal our God, King of the universe, creator of the fruit of the vine.

Father: Now we say the blessing that reminds us of the transitory nature of existence, of the continuous wonder of being alive. The she-hecheyanu.

ALL

בָּרוּךְ אַתָּה יְיָ, אֱלֹהֵינוּ מֶלֶךְ הָעוֹלָם, שֶׁהֶחֱיָנוּ, וְקִיְּמָנוּ, וְהִגִּיעָנוּ לַזְּמַן הַזֶּה.

Baruch Atah Adonai, Elohaynu Melech ha-olam, she-hecheyanu, v'ki-y'manu, v'higi-anu la-z'man ha-zeh.

Blessed art Thou, Eternal our God, King of the universe, who hast given us life, and kept us alive, and brought us to this moment.

All drink the first cup.

Father: Even before the Exodus from Egypt, our people each spring celebrated creation and the mystery of life. We remind ourselves that both the tender greens of the earth and the salts of the sea were joined together to sustain life. We remind ourselves that in slavery the brine of tears released our strength to survive.

Like all people, our people in ancient, pastoral times celebrated the liberation of the earth itself from wintry darkness, and rejoiced in the yearly rebirth of nature. This is beautifully described in Solomon's Song of Songs.

Life and growth of earth and sea, combined to give us sustenance. The coral reefs of Elath

MOTHER

For, lo, the winter is past,
The rain is over and gone;
The flowers appear on the earth;
The time of singing is come,
And the voice of the turtle is heard in our land;
The fig-tree putteth forth her green figs,
And the vines in blossom give forth their fragrance.

Father distributes the portions of greens, and each person dips his greens in salt water. All recite the blessing following.

ALL

בָּרוּךְ אַתָּה יְיָ, אֱלֹהֵינוּ מֶלֶךְ הָעוֹלָם, בּוֹרֵא פְּרִי הָאֲדָמָה.

Baruch Atah Adonai, Elohaynu Melech ha-olam, boray p'ri ha-adamah.

Blessed art Thou, Eternal our God, King of the universe, creator of the fruit of the earth.

Father uncovers the ceremonial matzoth.

The Father displays the ceremonial matzoth

Father: Here before me are three matzoth. It is said they represent, first, the priests of the Temple, the Kohanim, second, the singers and servitors of the Temple, the Levi-im, and last, the congregation of Israel, the Yisraelim.

It is also said that two of these matzoth, the upper and lower, represent the loaves of shewbread on display in the Temple, while the third matzah, the middle one, symbolizes the paschal lamb. Since the Passover sanctification was no longer possible after the destruction of the Temple, a matzah, in addition to the bone, came to represent the lamb, for this matzah we shall later divide and eat. First, it is the custom to divide the matzah in two.

At a Kurdish Seder in Moshav Rahava, near Lachish, the symbolic middle matzah is broken into two parts for the afikomen

---

He breaks the middle matzah, and places one part back under the cover.

One part we keep here. The second part we shall hide, while the children close their eyes. This is called the afikomen, from a Greek word that means dessert. After the meal the children will hunt for it and the finder will be rewarded. When the hidden part is found, we will put the two halves together again, and this will be a sign that what is broken off is not really lost to our people, so long as our children remember and search. Each of us will then eat a bit of the ceremonial matzah, in place of the lamb of the days of the Temple.

The children close their eyes. The afikomen is hidden.
Father now holds aloft the plate with the uncovered matzoth.

Father : Now we repeat, in ancient Aramaic, the call to Passover.

ALL

הָא לַחְמָא עַנְיָא דִּי אֲכָלוּ אַבְהָתָנָא בְּאַרְעָא דְמִצְרָיִם.

Ha lachma an-yah di achalu avahatana b'ara d'Mitzrayim.

This is the bread of affliction that our forefathers ate in the land of Egypt.

כָּל דִּכְפִין יֵיתֵי וְיֵכֻל; כָּל דִּצְרִיךְ יֵיתֵי וְיִפְסַח.

Kol dichfin yaytay v'yaychul ; kol ditzrich yaytay v'yifsach.

Let all who are hungered, come and eat! Whoever is in need, come and celebrate the Passover.

הָשַׁתָּא הָכָא, לְשָׁנָה הַבָּאָה בְּאַרְעָא דְיִשְׂרָאֵל.

Ha-shata hacha, l'shanah ha-ba'ah b'ara d' Yisrael.

Now here, next year in the land of Israel.

הָשַׁתָּא עַבְדֵי, לְשָׁנָה הַבָּאָה בְּנֵי חוֹרִין.

Ha-shata avday, l'shanah ha-ba'ah b'nay chorin.

Now enslaved, next year sons of freedom.

Father sets down the matzah plate. The wineglasses are filled for the second cup.

Father: Even the youngest among us notices this flat bread among the symbols of the Seder. It is unleavened bread, called matzah. Now let the youngest ask the Four Questions, about the differences that mark this night.

At a Yemenite Seder in Israel, a son asks the Four Questions

YOUNGEST

מַה נִּשְׁתַּנָּה הַלַּיְלָה הַזֶּה מִכָּל הַלֵּילוֹת?

Mah nishtanah ha-lailah ha-zeh mi-kol ha-laylot?

What makes this night different from all other nights?

שֶׁבְּכָל הַלֵּילוֹת אָנוּ אוֹכְלִין חָמֵץ וּמַצָּה,
הַלַּיְלָה הַזֶּה כֻּלּוֹ מַצָּה.

She-b'chol ha-laylot anu ochlin chametz u'matzah.
Ha-lailah ha-zeh kulo matzah.

On all other nights we may eat bread or matzah,
But on this night only matzah.

שֶׁבְּכָל הַלֵּילוֹת אָנוּ אוֹכְלִין שְׁאָר יְרָקוֹת,
הַלַּיְלָה הַזֶּה מָרוֹר.

She-b'chol ha-laylot anu ochlin sh'ar y'rakot.
Ha-lailah ha-zeh maror.

On all other nights we eat all kinds of greens,
But on this night only bitter herbs.

שֶׁבְּכָל הַלֵּילוֹת אֵין אָנוּ מַטְבִּילִין אֲפִלּוּ פַּעַם אֶחָת,
הַלַּיְלָה הַזֶּה שְׁתֵּי פְעָמִים.

She-b'chol ha-laylot ayn anu matbilin afilu pa-am echat.
Ha-lailah ha-zeh sh'tay f'amim.

On all other nights we do not dip even once,
But on this night we dip twice.

שֶׁבְּכָל הַלֵּילוֹת אָנוּ אוֹכְלִין בֵּין יוֹשְׁבִין וּבֵין מְסֻבִּין,
הַלַּיְלָה הַזֶּה כֻּלָּנוּ מְסֻבִּין.

She-b'chol ha-laylot anu ochlin bayn yoshvin uvayn m'subin.
Ha-lailah ha-zeh kulanu m'subin.

On all other nights we eat sitting or reclining,
But on this night we all recline.

Father

עֲבָדִים הָיִינוּ לְפַרְעֹה בְּמִצְרָיִם.

Avadim hayinu l'Pharaoh b'Mitzrayim.

Because we were slaves to Pharaoh in Egypt.

ALL

עֲבָדִים הָיִינוּ לְפַרְעֹה בְּמִצְרָיִם. וַיּוֹצִיאֵנוּ יְיָ אֱלֹהֵינוּ
מִשָּׁם בְּיָד חֲזָקָה וּבִזְרוֹעַ נְטוּיָה.

Avadim hayinu l'Pharaoh b'Mitzrayim. V'yotsiaynu Adonai Elohaynu mi-shaam b'yaad chazaka oo-vizroah n'tooyah.

Because we were slaves to Pharaoh in Egypt, and the Eternal, our God, brought us forth from there with a mighty hand and an outstretched arm.

MOTHER

If the Holy One, Blessed be He, had not brought forth our ancestors from Egypt, then we, and our children, and our children's children might still be enslaved in Egypt.

Father: There are Four Questions and there are also four ways to ask them: the heedless, the foolish, the dull, and the wise. The heedless child asks, "What is this ceremony of *yours?*" as though it did not concern him as well. The foolish child asks only what happened, without wanting to know what it means. The dull child doesn't even see anything to ask about. But the wise child asks, "What is the meaning of each thing we do?"

ALL

Let us all be wise children here. For everything in the Seder has meaning Even if we were full of wisdom, venerable sages, even if we were all steeped in Torah, it would still be incumbent on us to recount the Exodus from Egypt and search every word.

Father: Our venerable sages really did try to discuss every possible meaning in every word of the story of the Exodus, and they became so excited that they lost all sense of time. A story about this came to be included in the Haggadah. In the days of the early Talmudists there were five noted rabbis holding a Seder in B'nai B'rak, which is a center of religious study in Israel even today. They kept up their excited discussion hour after hour, until their pupils ran in and cried, "Rabbi Eliezer! Rabbi Joshua! Rabbi Elazar ben Azaria! Rabbi Akiba! Rabbi Tarphon! It's dawn already! Time to say the morning Shema!"
We are not as wise as the five sages. But let us hear a wise answer to the first question.

Father indicates, in turn, those who give the four answers.

FIRST

You ask, why on this night do we eat only matzoth?
Avadim hayinu—we were slaves. We were slaves in the land of Egypt. Our ancestors in their flight from the house of bondage in Egypt did not have time to let the dough rise, so they baked flat bread, called matzah. The Bible tells us, "They were thrust out of Egypt and could not tarry, neither had they time to prepare themselves victuals." In memory of this, we eat only matzoth on Passover.

SECOND

Why on this night do we eat bitter herbs?
Avadim hayinu—we were slaves. We eat bitter herbs because the Egyptians made bitter the lives of our forefathers. The Bible tells us, "They made their lives bitter with hard bondage in mortar and brick, and in all manner of labor in the fields, and all their servitude was terribly severe."

THIRD

Why do we dip twice?
Avadim hayinu—we were slaves. The first time we dipped our greens to taste the brine of enslavement. But also, to remind ourselves of all life and growth, of earth and sea, combined through divine impetus to give us sustenance.

From the Dead Sea comes the salt of survival

The second time we shall dip in charoset, to remind ourselves of the mortar that our forefathers mixed as slaves to the Pharaohs in Egypt. But our charoset is a mixture of sweet apples, nuts, raisins, and wine, to show us that in their bitter time of slavery our forefathers hoped for the sweet delights of freedom.

FOURTH

Why do we recline at ease?
Avadim hayinu—we were slaves. We recline at ease to remind ourselves that like our ancestors we can overcome slavery and bondage, for each of us is self-enslaved, and each of us is free to become his own master.

Father holds up the egg from the Passover plate.

Father: After the escape from Egypt the Israelites came into their promised land, and built their Temple in Jerusalem. To the Temple they brought festival offerings, in thanksgiving for the fertility of their fields and flocks. This egg recalls such offerings. The egg is the symbol of life, and of growth and fruition.

Life, newly emerged from the egg, at Ma'agan

Father holds up the shank bone.

This shank bone is the reminder of the Passover lamb, of the Divine instruction to the Israelites in Egypt to sacrifice a lamb and mark their doorposts with its blood. This was a sign for the Angel of Death to pass over their houses and strike only Egyptians, to cause them to set free their slaves. Again we ask ourselves, how did we come to be slaves in Egypt?

Father indicates each one's turn as the storytelling goes around the table.

THE RECITATION

FIRST

The Bible tells us that in ancient times our ancestors dwelt "on the other side of the great river and lived among idol-worshipers." In the city of Ur, our patriarch Abraham was the first to understand that God is One, the Eternal. To worship God in freedom, Abraham had to flee the land of idolators.

SECOND

The Bible says, "I took your father Abraham from the other side of the great river and led him throughout all the land of Canaan." And it relates: And the Lord said to Abraham, "All the land that thou seest, to thee I will give it, and to thy seed forever."

"Abraham's herds grew fat in the land"

THIRD

Abraham's herds grew fat in the land, and God gave him Isaac. And Isaac's son Jacob had many sons, but his favorite was Joseph, who was sold by his jealous brothers to a caravan, and they brought Joseph to Egypt.

FOURTH

Joseph rose to become the Pharaoh's minister over all Egypt. He prepared storehouses with grain. When drought and famine fell on all the region, Joseph's brothers came to Egypt to buy food. He recognized them, and had them bring their families to Egypt. There the Hebrews lived and multiplied.

"drought and famine fell on all the region"

"There arose a new King over Egypt, who knew not Joseph"

NEXT

There arose a new King over Egypt who knew not Joseph. And he said unto his people, "Behold the children of Israel are too many and too might for us." He feared that in a war they might go against him. Therefore he se over them taskmasters to afflict them with their burdens. And they built for Pharaoh treasure cities, Pithon and Ramses. They were slaves.

NEXT

And to destroy this entire people, Pharaoh charged the Hebrews, "Every son that is born ye shall cast into the river."

NEXT

A woman of the tribe of Levi placed her infant son inside an ark of bulrushes by the river's bank. He was found by Pharaoh's daughter and she called him Moses.

NEXT

His sister had been watching, and she offered his mother as nursemaid. Thus Moses was raised knowing his own people.

NEXT

When Moses was grown he one day came on an Egyptian smiting a Hebrew, and he smote the Egyptian. Moses fled from the face of Pharaoh and dwelt in the land of Midian.

NEXT

One day as he was guarding sheep the voice of the Eternal spoke to him from a burning bush, saying, "I will send thee to Pharaoh that thou mayest bring forth my people the Children of Israel out of Egypt."

NEXT

Again and again Moses stood before Pharaoh, demanding "Let my people go." But Pharaoh's heart was hardened.

Father: And as it is written, "We cried unto the Lord the God of our Fathers and the Lord heard our voice and saw our affliction and our toil and our oppression."

ALL

And the Lord brought us out of Egypt with a mighty hand and with an outstretched arm and with great terror and with signs and wonders.

"And the Lord brought us out of Egypt"

Father: Plague after plague was sent upon the Egyptians. In compassion and sorrow over the evil and suffering that exists in the world, our ancestors, in numbering the plagues, poured away with each word a drop of their wine of rejoicing. Rabbi Yehuda used only the initial for each plague, and made three words.

ALL

דְּצַ"ךְ, עֲדַ"שׁ, בְּאַחַ"ב.

D'tsach adash b'achav.

Each pours three drops of wine into a saucer.

Father: Or, we may recall the Ten Plagues.

If the plagues are read out, each pours a drop of wine as each plague is recalled.

ALL

דָּם

Dahm

Blood

צְפַרְדֵּעַ

Ts'fardaya

Frogs

כִּנִּים

Kinim

Vermin

עָרוֹב

Arov

Beasts

דֶּבֶר

Dever

Cattle Disease

שְׁחִין

Sh'chin

Boils

בָּרָד

Barad

Hail

אַרְבֶּה

Arbeh

Locusts

חֹשֶׁךְ

Choshech

Darkness

מַכַּת בְּכוֹרוֹת.

Makat b'chorot

Striking the First-Born

Sabhat Bar Daweel,
favored by archeologists as the crossing site

"They baked their bread in haste"

Father: When even the Pharaoh's own first-born son was stricken in the final plague, Pharaoh arose in the night and called for Moses and commanded him, "Get you forth from among my people!" In great haste the Children of Israel departed, as it is written, "They baked their bread in haste for they could not tarry." When they came to the Red Sea, Pharaoh again broke his word, for his chariots pursued them.

FIRST

The Lord caused the waters to be divided and the Israelites passed over safely; then the waters closed on the Egyptians, with their chariots of war. Thus the Children of Israel became free.

MOTHER

But as with the Ten Plagues, there is a story in our tradition about the Egyptians who drowned: When the Israelites crossed over safely, the

angels in Heaven began to sing in praise of God. But God looked down on the waters closing over the Egyptians, and cried, "How can you sing, when my children are drowning?"

ALL

Let us remember and never forget.

עֲבָדִים הָיִינוּ לְפַרְעֹה בְּמִצְרָיִם. וַיּוֹצִיאֵנוּ יְיָ אֱלֹהֵינוּ
מִשָּׁם בְּיָד חֲזָקָה וּבִזְרוֹעַ נְטוּיָה.

Avadim hayinu l'Pharaoh b'Mitzrayim. V'yotsiaynu Adonai Elohaynu mi-shaam b'yaad chazakah oo-vizroah n'tooyah.

Slaves were we to Pharaoh in Egypt, and the Eternal, our God, brought us out from there with a mighty hand and an outstretched arm.

וְאִלּוּ לֹא הוֹצִיא הַקָּדוֹשׁ בָּרוּךְ הוּא אֶת־אֲבוֹתֵינוּ
מִמִּצְרַיִם הֲרֵי אָנוּ וּבָנֵינוּ וּבְנֵי בָנֵינוּ מְשֻׁעְבָּדִים
הָיִינוּ לְפַרְעֹה בְּמִצְרָיִם.

V'iylu lo hotsi ha-Kadosh Baruch Hu et ahvotaynu mi-Mitzrayim haray anu oovahnaynu oov'nai vahnaynu m'shoobadim hayinu l'Pharaoh b'Mitzrayim.

If the Holy One, blessed be He, had not brought forth our ancestors from Egypt, then we, and our children, and our children's children might still be enslaved in Egypt.

Father: Let us remember and never forget: The promise of the Eternal to deliver our people has been kept again and again, through the ages.

FIRST

Blessed be He who kept his promise to Israel. For it was forethought by the Holy One, to fulfill what he had declared to our father Abraham along with the covenant: And he said to Abraham, "Know for a certainty that thy seed shall be strangers in a land that is not theirs, and shall serve them, and that people shall afflict them during four hundred years. And that nation whom they serve, them also will I judge! And afterwards the afflicted shall go forth with great substance."

All raise their wine cups.

SECOND

This is the promise that has sustained our ancestors and ourselves.

ALL

שֶׁלֹּא אֶחָד בִּלְבָד עָמַד עָלֵינוּ לְכַלּוֹתֵינוּ. אֶלָּא
שֶׁבְּכָל־דּוֹר וָדוֹר עוֹמְדִים עָלֵינוּ לְכַלּוֹתֵינוּ.
וְהַקָּדוֹשׁ בָּרוּךְ הוּא מַצִּילֵנוּ מִיָּדָם:

Sheh-lo echad bilvaad amaad aleynu l'chaalotaynu, elah sh'b'chol dor v'dor ohmdim ahlaynu l'chaalotaynu. V'ha-Kadosh Baruch Hu matsilaynu mi-yaadahm.

For not one only has risen against us to destroy us, but in every generation some have risen up against us to annihilate us. But the Holy One, Blessed be He, is our deliverer out of their hands.

Father

בְּכָל־דּוֹר וָדוֹר חַיָּב אָדָם לִרְאוֹת אֶת־עַצְמוֹ
כְּאִלּוּ הוּא יָצָא מִמִּצְרָיִם.

B'chol dor v'dor chayav adam liyrot et atsmoh k'iylu hu yaatsa mi-Mitzrayim.

In every generation each individual is bound to consider himself as if he in his own person had gone forth out of Egypt.

שֶׁנֶּאֱמַר וְהִגַּדְתָּ לְבִנְךָ בַּיּוֹם הַהוּא לֵאמֹר

She-ne-emar, v'higad'ta l'vincha b'yom ha-hu laymor

For it is written, on that day thou shalt tell thy son:

ALL

בַּעֲבוּר זֶה עָשָׂה יְיָ לִי בְּצֵאתִי מִמִּצְרָיִם:

Ba-avoor zeh aasah Adonai li b'tsayti mi-Mitzrayim

This is because of what the Eternal did for *me* when *I* came out of Egypt.

לְפִיכָךְ אֲנַחְנוּ חַיָּבִים לְהוֹדוֹת לְהַלֵּל לְשַׁבֵּחַ לְפָאֵר
לְרוֹמֵם לְהַדֵּר לְבָרֵךְ לְעַלֵּה וּלְקַלֵּס לְמִי שֶׁעָשָׂה
לַאֲבוֹתֵינוּ וְלָנוּ אֶת־כָּל־הַנִּסִּים הָאֵלֶּה.

L'fiychach ahnachnuh chayavim l'hodoth l'haalel l'shabeyach l'fa'aur l'rohmaym l'hadayr l'varaych l'ahlay oo-l'kahlays l-mi sheh-aasah l'ahvotaynu v-lahnu et kol ha-nissim ha-ayleh.

We are therefore duty bound to thank, praise, laud, glorify, extol, honor, bless, exalt, and revere Him who wrought all these wonders for our ancestors and for us.

הוֹצִיאָנוּ מֵעַבְדוּת לְחֵרוּת. מִיָּגוֹן לְשִׂמְחָה. מֵאֵבֶל
לְיוֹם טוֹב. וּמֵאֲפֵלָה לְאוֹר גָּדוֹל. וּמִשִּׁעְבּוּד לִגְאֻלָּה
וְנֹאמַר לְפָנָיו שִׁירָה חֲדָשָׁה: הַלְלוּיָהּ.

Ho-tsiyanu mayavduth l'chayrut. Mi-yahgun l'simcha. May-ayvel l'yom tov. Oo-may-aafaylah l'ohr gaadol. Oomi-shiybood lig'oolah v'nomar l'fanaav shirah chadashah : Halleluyah.

He brought us forth from bondage to freedom, from sorrow to joy, from mourning to festivity, from darkness to bright light, and from servitude to redemption. Therefore let us sing before him a new song! Halleluyah!

בָּרוּךְ אַתָּה יְיָ, אֱלֹהֵינוּ מֶלֶךְ הָעוֹלָם, אֲשֶׁר גְּאָלָנוּ
וְגָאַל אֶת־אֲבוֹתֵינוּ מִמִּצְרַיִם וְהִגִּיעָנוּ לַלַּיְלָה הַזֶּה
לֶאֱכָל־בּוֹ מַצָּה וּמָרוֹר: כֵּן יְיָ אֱלֹהֵינוּ וֵאלֹהֵי
אֲבוֹתֵינוּ יַגִּיעֵנוּ לְמוֹעֲדִים וְלִרְגָלִים אֲחֵרִים הַבָּאִים
לִקְרָאתֵנוּ לְשָׁלוֹם שְׂמֵחִים בְּבִנְיַן עִירֶךָ וְשָׂשִׂים
בַּעֲבוֹדָתֶךָ. וְנֹאכַל שָׁם מִן הַזְּבָחִים וּמִן הַפְּסָחִים
אֲשֶׁר יַגִּיעַ דָּמָם עַל קִיר מִזְבַּחֲךָ לְרָצוֹן. וְנוֹדֶה
לְךָ שִׁיר חָדָשׁ עַל גְּאֻלָּתֵנוּ וְעַל פְּדוּת נַפְשֵׁנוּ.
בָּרוּךְ אַתָּה יְיָ גָּאַל יִשְׂרָאֵל:

Baruch Atah Adonai Elohaynu Melech ha-olam asher g'alanu v'ga-al et avotaynu mi-Mitzrayim v'higiyanu lalayla hazeh le-echol boh matzah oo-maror. Kayn Adonai Elohaynu v'Elohay avotaynu yagiayynu l'mo-adim v'l'regalim aachayrim ha-baa'im likrataynu l'shalom smaychim b-vinyaan ihrcha v'saasim ba-avodatecha. V'nochal shahm min ha-zvachim oomin ha-psachim asher yagiyah dahmam ahl kir mizbachacha l'ratzohn. V'nodeh l'cha shir chadash al g'oolataynu v'ahl p'dooth nahfshaynu. Baruch Atah Adonai gaal Yisrael.

Blessed art Thou, Lord God, King of the universe, who delivered us and delivered our fathers from Egypt, and brought us to this night to eat matzah and bitter herbs. So, too, Lord our God and God of our fathers, bring us to future observances and feasts, in peace, that we may happily rebuild Thy city and rejoice in Thy service. There shall we sing Thee a new song for our deliverance and for the redemption of our souls. Blessed art Thou, Lord, who redeemed Israel!

Father: Now these are the psalms that were sung in the Temple at Passover.

He indicates those who shall recite, in Hebrew or English.

FIRST

הַלְלוּיָהּ!
הַלְלוּ, עַבְדֵי יְיָ,
הַלְלוּ אֶת שֵׁם יְיָ.
יְהִי שֵׁם יְיָ מְבֹרָךְ,
מֵעַתָּה וְעַד עוֹלָם.
מִמִּזְרַח שֶׁמֶשׁ עַד מְבוֹאוֹ,
מְהֻלָּל שֵׁם יְיָ.
רָם עַל כָּל גּוֹיִם יְיָ,
עַל הַשָּׁמַיִם כְּבוֹדוֹ.
מִי כַּייָ אֱלֹהֵינוּ,
הַמַּגְבִּיהִי לָשָׁבֶת.
הַמַּשְׁפִּילִי לִרְאוֹת
בַּשָּׁמַיִם וּבָאָרֶץ?
מְקִימִי מֵעָפָר דָּל,
מֵאַשְׁפֹּת יָרִים אֶבְיוֹן.
לְהוֹשִׁיבִי עִם נְדִיבִים,
עִם נְדִיבֵי עַמּוֹ.
מוֹשִׁיבִי עֲקֶרֶת הַבַּיִת,
אֵם הַבָּנִים שְׂמֵחָה;
הַלְלוּיָהּ!

Halleluyah!
Hallaloo avday Adonai
Hallaloo et shem Adonai

Y'hiy shem Adonai m'vorach
Me-atah v'ahd olam.
Mimizrach shemesh ahd m'vo-oh
M'hoolal shem Adonai.
Rahm ahl kol goyim Adonai
Ahl ha-shamayim k'vodoh.
Miy k'Adonai Elohaynu
Ha-magbiyhiy lashavet.
Hamashpiliy liyrot
Bashamayim oo-va-aretz?
M'kiymiy me-ahfar dahl
Me-ashpoht yarim evyon.
L'hoshiviy im n'divim
Im n'divey ahmoh.
Moshiviy akereth habayit
Aym habanim smaycha
Halleluyah!

Halleluyah!
Praise, O servants of the Lord,
Praise the Name of the Lord!
The Name of the Lord be blessed
From now to eternity!
From the sun's rising to its going down
Hail the name of the Lord!

Above all nations is the Lord
Above the heavens is His glory.
Who is like unto the Lord our God
Who is seated so high,
That in the same gaze He encompasses
What is in Heaven and on Earth!

He raises the poor out of the dust
The needy out of the dung
To seat them among princes,
Among princes of His people.
The barren housewife He brings forth
As a happy mother of sons!
Halleluyah!

SECOND

בְּצֵאת יִשְׂרָאֵל מִמִּצְרָיִם,
בֵּית יַעֲקֹב מֵעַם לֹעֵז.
הָיְתָה יְהוּדָה לְקָדְשׁוֹ,

יִשְׂרָאֵל מַמְשְׁלוֹתָיו.
הַיָּם רָאָה וַיָּנֹס;
הַיַּרְדֵּן יִסֹּב לְאָחוֹר.
הֶהָרִים רָקְדוּ כְאֵילִים,
גְּבָעוֹת כִּבְנֵי צֹאן.
מַה לְּךָ הַיָּם כִּי תָנוּס?
הַיַּרְדֵּן, תִּסֹּב לְאָחוֹר?
הֶהָרִים, תִּרְקְדוּ כְאֵילִים;
גְּבָעוֹת, כִּבְנֵי צֹאן?
מִלִּפְנֵי אָדוֹן חוּלִי אָרֶץ,
מִלִּפְנֵי אֱלוֹהַּ יַעֲקֹב.
הַהֹפְכִי הַצּוּר אֲגַם מָיִם,
חַלָּמִישׁ לְמַעְיְנוֹ מָיִם.

B'tsayt Yisrael Mitzrayim
Bayt Yaacov may-ahm lo-ayz
Haiy'tah Yehuda l'kodsho
Yisrael mahm'sh-lotav.
Hayam ra-ah va-yanos
Ha-Yardayn yisov l'achor
He-harim rakdoo ch'aylim
G'va-oth kiv'nai tson
Mah l'chȧ hayam kiy tanoos!
Ha-Yardayn tisov l'achor!
He-harim tir'kdoo ch'aylim!
G'va-oth kiv'nai tson!
Milifnay Adon chooli aretz
Milifnay Eloah Yaacov.
Hahofchiy hatsoor aagam mayim
Chalaamish l'maa-inooh mayim.

When Israel came forth out of Egypt,
The House of Jacob from a strange-tongued people,
Then Israel became God's sanctuary,
Judah, His dominion.
The sea beheld, and fled!
The Jordan turned backward!

The mountains leaped like rams,
The hills like lambs!
What's come over you, O sea, that you flee!
And you, Jordan, that you turn backward!
You mountains, that leap like rams,
You hills, like lambs!
Tremble, earth,
Before the Lord,
Before the God of Jacob!
He who turned the rock into a pool of water
The flint rock into fountains of water!

"From the sun's rising to its going down, hail the name of the Lord!"

"You hills, like lambs"

Father: From the Red Sea, Moses led Israel inland. They crossed the desert and dwelt for a time in the oasis of Kadesh Barnea, that has been identified in our time. They lived in tents, and booths made of reeds, as Bedouin do to this day. Early in their wandering they came into the wilderness of Sinai, and encamped, and Moses went up on the Mount, where he received God's commandments. Let us repeat the Ten Commandments.

"They lived in booths made of reeds," still found among the Bedouin

The oasis of Kadesh Barnea

ALL

I am the Lord thy God, who brought thee out of the land of Egypt, out of the house of bondage.
Thou shalt have no other gods before Me.
Thou shalt not make unto thee a graven image . . . thou shalt not bow down unto them, nor serve them.
Thou shalt not take the name of the Lord thy God in vain.
Remember the Sabbath day, to keep it holy.
Honor thy father and thy mother.
Thou shalt not murder.
Thou shalt not commit adultery.
Thou shalt not steal.
Thou shalt not bear false witness against thy neighbor.
Thou shalt not covet.

Father : This is the word of God as embodied in our Torah. Let us drink the second cup.

ALL

בָּרוּךְ אַתָּה יְיָ, אֱלֹהֵינוּ מֶלֶךְ הָעוֹלָם, בּוֹרֵא פְּרִי הַגָּפֶן.

Baruch Atah Adonai, Elohaynu Melech ha-olam, boray p'ri ha-gafen.

Blessed art Thou, Eternal our God, King of the universe, creator of the fruit of the vine.

All drink the second cup.

Father : We are now coming to the Seder meal. As we ordinarily begin with the breaking of bread, we begin tonight with the breaking of matzah.

Father breaks off, for each, a small portion of the ceremonial matzah.

ALL

בָּרוּךְ אַתָּה יְיָ, אֱלֹהֵינוּ מֶלֶךְ הָעוֹלָם, הַמּוֹצִיא לֶחֶם מִן הָאָרֶץ.

Baruch Atah Adonai, Elohaynu Melech ha-olam, ha-motzi lechem min ha-aretz.

Blessed art Thou, Eternal our God, King of the universe, who bringest forth bread from the earth.

בָּרוּךְ אַתָּה יְיָ, אֱלֹהֵינוּ מֶלֶךְ הָעוֹלָם, אֲשֶׁר קִדְּשָׁנוּ בְּמִצְוֹתָיו, וְצִוָּנוּ עַל אֲכִילַת מַצָּה.

Baruch Atah Adonai, Elohaynu Melech ha-olam, asher kid'shanu b'mitzvotav, v'tzivahnu al achilat matzah.

Blessed art Thou, Eternal our God, King of the universe, who hast sanctified us through Thy commandments and instructed us to eat unleavened bread.

All eat part of their portion of the ceremonial matzah, representing the paschal lamb, saving a piece for the "Hillel sandwich" to come.

Father: Now each will take a bit of the bitter herb and dip it in charoset to fulfill the commandment of this night to eat the bitter herb. Thus, we dip our food the second time.

If the horseradish is in slices, place a bit of charoset on a slice; if it is ground, place some on a spoon, together with charoset.

ALL

בָּרוּךְ אַתָּה יְיָ, אֱלֹהֵינוּ מֶלֶךְ הָעוֹלָם, אֲשֶׁר קִדְּשָׁנוּ בְּמִצְוֹתָיו, וְצִוָּנוּ עַל אֲכִילַת מָרוֹר.

Baruch Atah Adonai, Elohaynu Melech ha-olam, asher kid'shanu b'mitzvotav, v'tzivahnu al achilat maror.

"and Moses went up on the Mount"

Blessed art Thou, Eternal our God, King of the universe, who hast sanctified us through Thy commandments and instructed us to eat bitter herbs.

Father: Tradition adds one more custom, in honor of the great teacher, Hillel, head of the rabbinic academy in Jerusalem in the time of the Romans. A heathen asked the rabbi to teach him the entire Torah while he stood on one foot. Hillel said, "Do not unto others what you would hate them to do unto you. That is the whole Torah," he told the man, "the rest is commentary. Now go and study." On Passover, Hillel followed precisely the instruction about the sanctified lamb. "Upon unleavened bread and bitter herbs shall they eat it." So he placed a bit of the paschal offering on the matzah, with bitter herbs. In remembrance of the Temple and Hillel, we shall place the bitter herb on the matzah in place of the paschal lamb.

All eat the matzah with bitter herbs.

Father: The teaching is completed and we may come to the meal. It was a grandson of Rabbi Hillel, Rabbi Gamaliel, who gave us the rule for when we may eat the meal. "He who has not talked about these three things," he said, "has not fulfilled the obligation to observe the Passover. They are: the shank bone, the matzah, and the maror."

We have explained all three, so let us begin the Passover feast!

The ceremonial Passover plate is removed.

THE MEAL IS SERVED

A PORTFOLIO OF ISRAELI SEDERS

Celebrating their Passover as Israelis are Jews from Kurdistan, from Europe, from Bokhara, from seventy lands. In the family Seder at home, they continue their traditional observances, while in the larger family of the kibbutz, the ancient and modern ways are often combined. To recall the Exodus, a Bokharan wraps the afikomen in a silk kerchief and takes it on his back. In the kibbutz, the children carry emblems of spring through the hall, and chant the Four Questions in chorus.

Jews from Yemen

כרמליה

A family from Bokhara

הגדה
של
פסח

Author Meyer Levin roasting the traditional Passover lamb in the age-old setting of Israel's Red Sea shore

A kibbutz seder

After the first course is a good time to recite, chant, or sing the traditional "Dayenu," which means, "It would have been enough for us." The verses go around the table, each person doing a line, all joining in the refrain. First may come the recitation, then the song.

Father: How many wonders did the Eternal perform for us?

FIRST

If He had brought us out of Egypt but had not punished our enemies—

ALL

Dayenu!

SECOND

If He had split the sea for us but had not drowned our pursuers—

ALL

Dayenu!

THIRD

If He had saved us from our pursuers but had not fed us manna in the desert—

ALL

Dayenu!

FOURTH

If He had fed us manna in the desert but had not given us the Sabbath—

"Manna," found on the haloxylon and other plants

ALL

Dayenu!

NEXT

If He had given us the Sabbath but had not given us the Torah—

ALL

Dayenu!

NEXT

If He had given us the Torah but had not brought us into Israel—

ALL

Dayenu!

NEXT

If He had brought us into Israel but had not built His Temple—

ALL

Dayenu! Dayenu! Dayenu!

I - lu ho - tsi, ho - tsi - a - nu, ho - tsi - a - nu mi - Mits - ra - yim,

Ho - tsi - a - nu mi Mitsra yim, Da- ye - nu: Da - da - ye - nu,____

da - da - ye nu,____ da - da ye nu, da - ye - da - ye - nu____ yenu, daye nu:

אִלּוּ הוֹצִיאָנוּ מִמִּצְרַיִם, דַּיֵּנוּ.
אִלּוּ נָתַן לָנוּ אֶת הַשַּׁבָּת, דַּיֵּנוּ.
אִלּוּ נָתַן לָנוּ אֶת הַתּוֹרָה, דַּיֵּנוּ.
אִלּוּ הִכְנִיסָנוּ לְאֶרֶץ יִשְׂרָאֵל, דַּיֵּנוּ.

Had He brought us out of Egypt
Only brought us out of Egypt
Had he brought us out of Egypt
Dayenu!
Had He given us the Sabbath
Also given us the Sabbath
Dayenu!
Had He brought us into Israel
Also brought us into Israel
Dayenu!

At the end of the meal, the third cup is filled.

Father : We have eaten our Passover meal as free men. Let us give thanks to the source of all life and freedom. We will say grace.

ALL

בָּרוּךְ שֶׁאָכַלְנוּ מִשֶּׁלּוֹ וּבְטוּבוֹ חָיִינוּ.

Baruch she-achalnu mi'shelo u-v'tuvo chayinu.

Blessed is the Eternal through whose bounty we have been fed and through whose love we are given life.

Father

בָּרוּךְ הוּא וּבָרוּךְ שְׁמוֹ.

Baruch Hu uvaruch Sh'mo.

Blessed be He and blessed His Name.

ALL

יְהִי שֵׁם יְיָ מְבֹרָךְ מֵעַתָּה וְעַד עוֹלָם.

Y'hi Shaym Adonai m'vorach may-ata v'ad olam.

May the Name of God be blessed from now to eternity.

בָּרוּךְ אַתָּה יְיָ, אֱלֹהֵינוּ מֶלֶךְ הָעוֹלָם, הַזָּן אֶת־
הָעוֹלָם כֻּלּוֹ בְּטוּבוֹ בְּחֵן בְּחֶסֶד וּבְרַחֲמִים הוּא
נוֹתֵן לֶחֶם לְכָל־בָּשָׂר כִּי לְעוֹלָם חַסְדּוֹ:

Baruch Atah Adonai, Elohaynu Melech ha-olam, hazan et ha-olam kooloh b'toovoh b'chayn b'chesed oo-v'rachamim, hoo notayn lechem l'chol basar kiy l'olam chasdoh.

Blessed art Thou, Eternal our God, King of the universe, who feedest the whole world. With goodness, with grace, and with kindness and mercy, He giveth food to every creature, for His mercy endureth forever.

MOTHER

וּבְטוּבוֹ הַגָּדוֹל תָּמִיד לֹא חָסַר־לָנוּ וְאַל יֶחְסַר־
לָנוּ מָזוֹן לְעוֹלָם וָעֶד בַּעֲבוּר שְׁמוֹ הַגָּדוֹל:

Oo-v'toovoh ha-gadol taamid lo chasar-laanu v'ahl yechsar laanu maazohn l'olam va-ed, ba-avur shmo hagadol.

And in His great goodness we have never been in want, so, in His great Name, may there never be want of sustenance, to the end of time.

YOUNGEST

כִּי הוּא זָן וּמְפַרְנֵס לַכֹּל וּמֵטִיב לַכֹּל וּמֵכִין מָזוֹן
לְכָל־בְּרִיּוֹתָיו אֲשֶׁר בָּרָא.

Kih Hu zahn oo-m'farness lakol oo-maytiv lakol oo-maychin maazohn lakol briyo-tahv asher barah.

For He feeds and provides for all, and is good to all, and prepares food for all the creatures He has created.

ALL

בָּרוּךְ אַתָּה יְיָ, הַזָּן אֶת־הַכֹּל.

Baruch Atah Adonai, ha-zan et ha-kol.

Blessed art Thou, Lord, who feedest all.

Father :

נוֹדֶה לְּךָ יְיָ אֱלֹהֵינוּ עַל שֶׁהִנְחַלְתָּ לַאֲבוֹתֵינוּ אֶרֶץ

חֶמְדָּה טוֹבָה וּרְחָבָה וְעַל שֶׁהוֹצֵאתָנוּ יְיָ אֱלֹהֵינוּ
מֵאֶרֶץ מִצְרַיִם וּפְדִיתָנוּ מִבֵּית עֲבָדִים

Nodeh l'cha Adonai Elohaynu ahl shehinchaltah l'avotaynu eretz chemda tovah oor'chavah v'ahl she-hotsaytanu Adonai Elohaynu may-eretz Mitzrayim oo-f'diytanu mi-bayt avadim.

We give thanks unto Thee, Lord our God, for that pleasant, goodly, and ample land which Thou wast pleased to cause our ancestors to inherit, and because, Eternal our God, Thou hast brought us forth from the land of Egypt and redeemed us from the house of bondage.

FIRST

וְעַל בְּרִיתְךָ שֶׁחָתַמְתָּ בִּבְשָׂרֵנוּ וְעַל תּוֹרָתְךָ
שֶׁלִּמַּדְתָּנוּ

V'ahl brit-cha sheh-chatamta bivsahraynu v'ahl Torat-cha sheh-limad'tanu.

And on Thy covenant which Thou hast sealed in our flesh, and for Thy Torah which Thou hast taught us.

ALL

וְעַל הַכֹּל יְיָ אֱלֹהֵינוּ אֲנַחְנוּ מוֹדִים לָךְ וּמְבָרְכִים
אוֹתָךְ

V'ahl ha-kol Adonai Elohaynu anachnu modim lach oo-m'vrahchim otach.

And for all these things, Lord our God, we thank Thee and praise Thee.

SECOND

רַחֵם יְיָ אֱלֹהֵינוּ עַל־יִשְׂרָאֵל עַמֶּךָ וְעַל יְרוּשָׁלַיִם
עִירֶךָ וְעַל צִיּוֹן מִשְׁכַּן כְּבוֹדֶךָ

Raachem Adonai Elohaynu ahl-Yisrael amecha v'ahl Yerushalayim ihrecha v'ahl Ziyohn mishkan k'vodecha.

Have compassion, Eternal our God, on Israel Thy people, on Jerusalem Thy city, and on Zion the abode of Thy glory.

ALL

וְהַרְוַח־לָנוּ יְיָ אֱלֹהֵינוּ מְהֵרָה מִכָּל־צָרוֹתֵינוּ: וְנָא אַל־תַּצְרִיכֵנוּ יְיָ אֱלֹהֵינוּ לֹא לִידֵי מַתְּנַת בָּשָׂר וָדָם וְלֹא לִידֵי הַלְוָאָתָם כִּי אִם לְיָדְךָ הַמְּלֵאָה הַפְּתוּחָה הַקְּדוֹשָׁה וְהָרְחָבָה שֶׁלֹּא נֵבוֹשׁ וְלֹא נִכָּלֵם לְעוֹלָם וָעֶד:

V'harvach lanu Adonai Elohaynu m'hayra mikol tsarotaynu. V'nah ahl tatsrichaynu Adonai Elohaynu lo liyday matnat basaar v'dahm v-lo liyday halvaatam kiy ihm l'yaadcha ha-mlayah ha-ptoocha ha-kdoosha v'ha-r'chava sheh-lo nayvosh v'lo nikalaym l'olam va-ed.

And deliver us, Lord our God, speedily from all our troubles, and leave not our needs, O Eternal our God, to gifts at the hands of flesh and blood, nor to their loans, but only to Thy full, open, holy, and ample hand, so that, forevermore, we need not feel ashamed or demeaned.

THIRD

זָכְרֵנוּ יְיָ אֱלֹהֵינוּ בּוֹ לְטוֹבָה. וּפָקְדֵנוּ בוֹ לִבְרָכָה. וְהוֹשִׁיעֵנוּ בוֹ לְחַיִּים.

Zachraynu Adonai Elohaynu boh l'tovah, oofukdaynu voh livrachah. V'hoshiaynu voh l'chayim.

Remember us, Lord our God, this day for the good. Bestow Thy blessing upon us and save us to enjoy life!

ALL

שְׁפֹךְ חֲמָתְךָ עַל־מַמְלָכוֹת אֲשֶׁר בְּשִׁמְךָ לֹא קָרָאוּ:

Sh'foch chamatcha ahl mamlachot asher b'Shimcha lo kara-oo.

Pour out Thy wrath upon the oppressors who do not heed the Divine Name.

Father

עֹשֶׂה שָׁלוֹם בִּמְרוֹמָיו הוּא יַעֲשֶׂה שָׁלוֹם עָלֵינוּ וְעַל כָּל־יִשְׂרָאֵל. וְאִמְרוּ אָמֵן:

Oseh shalom bim'romav, Hu ya-aseh shalom alaynu v'ahl kol Yisrael, v-imroo Omayn.

May He who maketh peace in all His vastness grant peace unto us, and all Israel, and all mankind, and let us say Amen.

ALL

אָמֵן:

Omayn.

Amen.

וּבְנֵה יְרוּשָׁלַיִם עִיר הַקֹּדֶשׁ בִּמְהֵרָה בְיָמֵינוּ. בָּרוּךְ אַתָּה יְיָ, בּוֹנֵה בְרַחֲמָיו יְרוּשָׁלָיִם, אָמֵן.

Oo-v'nay Yerushalayim ihr ha-kodesh bim'hayrah v'yomaynu. Baruch Atah Adonai, boneh v'rachamav Yerushalayim. Omayn.

O build Jerusalem, the Holy City, speedily, in our days. Blessed art Thou, O Eternal, who in Thy compassion buildest Jerusalem. Amen.

Father

הָרַחֲמָן. הוּא יִשְׁלַח בְּרָכָה מְרֻבָּה בַּבַּיִת הַזֶּה וְעַל שֻׁלְחָן זֶה שֶׁאָכַלְנוּ עָלָיו:

Ha-rachaman Hu yishlach brachah m'roobah ba-bayit hazeh v'ahl shulchan zeh she-achalnu alahv.

May He who is most compassionate send abundant blessings on this house and on this table on which we have eaten.

ALL

הָרַחְמָן. הוּא יְבָרֵךְ אֶת הַבַּיִת הַזֶּה

Ha-rachaman. Hu y'varaych et ha-bayit ha-zeh.

May He who is most compassionate bless this house.

FATHER, MOTHER (*to the grandparents*)

הָרַחֲמָן, הוּא יְבָרֵךְ אֶת אָבִי מוֹרִי וְאֶת אִמִּי מוֹרָתִי

Ha-rachaman. Hu y'varaych et avi mohri v'et iymi mohrati.

May He who is most compassionate bless my father who taught me, and my mother who taught me.

EACH (*according to relationship, turning to those to be blessed*)

וְאֶת אִשְׁתִּי

V'et ishti.

And my wife.

וְאֶת בַּעְלִי

V'et baali.

And my husband.

וְאֶת זַרְעִי

V'et zaari.

And my children.

ALL

הָרַחֲמָן, הוּא יְבָרֵךְ אֶת כָּל הַמְּסֻבִּין כַּאן, אוֹתָם
וְאֶת זַרְעָם וְאֶת כָּל אֲשֶׁר לָהֶם.

Ha-rachaman. Hu y'varaych et kol ha-m'soobiyn cahn, ohtam, v'et zaaram v'et kol asher lahem.

May He who is most compassionate bless all who are gathered here—them, their families, and all that is theirs.

MOTHER

הָרַחֲמָן. הוּא יְזַכֵּנוּ לִימוֹת הַמָּשִׁיחַ

Ha-rachaman. Hu yizakaynu l'iymot ha-Mashiach.

May He who is most compassionate make us worthy to behold the day of Messiah.

Father: We drink the third cup!

ALL

בָּרוּךְ אַתָּה יְיָ, אֱלֹהֵינוּ מֶלֶךְ הָעוֹלָם, בּוֹרֵא פְּרִי
הַגָּפֶן.

Baruch Atah Adonai, Elohaynu Melech ha-olam, boray p'ri ha-gafen.

Blessed art Thou, Eternal our God, King of the universe, creator of the fruit of the vine.

Each drinks his third cup.
The wine is poured for the fourth cup.
The cup of Elijah is filled.

Cup of Elijah, nineteenth-century Bohemian crystal (Iṣrael Museum, Jerusalem)

Father : We are told that Elijah the Prophet visits every house where a Seder is being held.

He selects someone to open the door.

Let us open the door for Elijah, and also as a symbol of hospitality and friendliness, as a sign that none is shut off from his fellow man.

הָרַחֲמָן. הוּא יִשְׁלַח לָנוּ אֶת־אֵלִיָּהוּ הַנָּבִיא זָכוּר
לַטּוֹב וִיבַשֶּׂר־לָנוּ בְּשׂוֹרוֹת טוֹבוֹת יְשׁוּעוֹת וְנֶחָמוֹת:

Ha-rachaman, Hu yishlach lanu et Eliyahu ha-navi zachur la-tov vivaser lanu b'soroth tovoth y'shuoth v'nechamoth.

May the Compassionate One send us Elijah the Prophet of blessed memory, to bring us good tidings of sympathy and salvation.

The Golden Gate for the Messiah in the old city wall of Jerusalem

In the cave of Elijah on Mount Carmel

The door has been opened.
Father indicates the cup of Elijah.

Father: This is the cup of Elijah the Prophet, for our legends tell us that Elijah enters every house where a Seder is taking place. Why Elijah? Of all our Biblical Prophets, it is Elijah who became the kindly mediator between Heaven and Earth. The Bible stories tell us of a fiery chariot sent to carry him up to Heaven. And from Heaven, he was to return to help prepare mankind for the dreamed-of time of the coming of the Messiah, the time of judgment and redemption. The Prophet Malachi foretold this about Elijah, when he said,

Behold, I will send you Elijah the Prophet
Before the coming of the great and terrible day of the Lord,
And he shall turn the hearts of the fathers to the children,
And the hearts of the children to their fathers.

In the centuries when our people suffered in the ghettos, they longed for this kind-hearted messenger of the millennium, and they told innumerable tales of how Elijah would instantly appear if a Jew in great trouble or danger called out, "Elijah! Help me!" In such stories, he would appear in different ways; sometimes he was a camel driver who rescued a traveler lost in the desert, sometimes he even flew through the air to rescue a Jew whom robbers had hurled off a mountain path. Or, he was a beggar passing in the street, to save the soul of a wealthy Jew who was suddenly dying, by giving him a last chance to perform an act of charity.

Elijah may come and go in different disguises, unrecognized, but the Jew who has called out, and been helped by him, somehow knows, "Elijah came."

The door is closed.

Now the children may hunt for the afikomen, and perhaps Elijah will help one of them to find it.

The children leave their seats to hunt for the afikomen. During this time, the cup of Elijah may be mysteriously drained.
While the hunt goes on, the song of Elijah is taken up.

אֵלִיָּהוּ הַנָּבִיא, אֵלִיָּהוּ הַתִּשְׁבִּי,
אֵלִיָּהוּ, אֵלִיָּהוּ, אֵלִיָּהוּ הַגִּלְעָדִי,
בִּמְהֵרָה בְיָמֵינוּ יָבֹא אֵלֵינוּ
עִם מָשִׁיחַ בֶּן דָּוִד, עִם מָשִׁיחַ בֶּן דָּוִ

Eliyahu of prophecy, Eliyahu the Tishbi,
Eliyahu, Eliyahu, Eliyahu from Giladi,
Come with speed and in our day
Come to us, O come to stay
With Messiah ben David, with Messiah ben David.

The child who has found the afikomen brings it to Father, who takes the other part of this matzah from the plate and holds up the two parts, matching them together.

Wailing Wall

In al Aqsa mosque

Near the Holy Sepulcher

Father: What is broken shall be made whole. What is shattered shall be restored. Our Messianic hope is in our children, to find what is lost, to bring together what is broken, to restore our faith.

While the afikomen is being distributed, all recite.

ALL

The Prophets teach us:
For in the end of days it shall come to pass
That the mountain of the Lord's house shall be established
As the top of the mountains,
And it shall be exalted above the hills.
Out of Zion shall go forth the Torah.
And the word of the Lord from Jerusalem.
And He shall judge between many peoples,
And shall decide concerning the mighty nations afar off.
They shall beat their swords into plowshares,
And their spears into pruning hooks.
Nation shall not lift up sword against nation,
Neither shall they learn war any more.
But they shall sit every man under his vine and fig tree
And none shall make them afraid,
For the mouth of the Lord of Hosts hath spoken.

The Torah teaches:
The stranger that sojourneth with thee in thy land, thou
shalt not wrong.
Thou shalt love him as thyself, for ye were strangers in the land of Egypt.
I am the Lord thy God.
Thou shalt not hate thy brother in thy heart.
Thou shalt love thy neighbor as thyself.
I am the Lord.

All eat the afikomen.

Father: We shall now commemorate our sacred dead.

All rise.

Masada

ALL

Let us remember and never forget the martyred Jews of all generations, the victims of the Romans, of the Inquisition, the victims of the Crusades, of pogroms, the six million who fell to the evil of a tyrant who sought to suppress the freedom of all mankind.
Let us remember and never forget those who gave the world an eternal example of human courage, the heroes of Masada, the Jews who fought in the ghettos and in the concentration camps, in the underground resistance armies and in the restoration of Israel, who proved that the human spirit cannot be destroyed.
Remember, and never forget their memory.

Father: Now raise the fourth cup. We shall hear the great Hallel, the concluding paean of praise.

All raise their cups.

MOTHER

The soul of all living shall bless Thy name, O Eternal our God!
Were our mouths filled with song as the sea is with water,
Were our tongues loud with exaltation as the roaring billows of the sea,
Were our words extended with praise like the widely extended skies,
Our eyes sparkling like the sun and the moon,
Our hands spread forth as the eagle's wing in the firmament,
Our feet as swift as the doe,
Yet would we be incapable of rendering sufficient thanks to
Thee, O Eternal, our God and God of our fathers,
Or to bless Thy name for even a thousandth part of the many thousands
and myriads of benefits which Thou hast conferred on Thy people.
Praised be Thy name forever, Thou Great, Holy and Sovereign God, in
Heaven and upon the Earth!

Father: Let us drink the fourth cup to the freedom of all!

A prayer of remembrance at the Wailing Wall

ALL

בָּרוּךְ אַתָּה יְיָ, אֱלֹהֵינוּ מֶלֶךְ הָעוֹלָם, בּוֹרֵא פְּרִי הַגָּפֶן.

Baruch Atah Adonai, Elohaynu Melech ha-olam, boray p'ri ha-gafen.

Blessed art Thou, Eternal our God, King of the universe, creator of the fruit of the vine.

ALL

Have compassion on us, O Eternal our God, and on Thy people Israel, on Jerusalem Thy City, on Zion the tabernacle of Thy glory. Bring peace and freedom to every people. For Thou, O Eternal, art good and beneficent to all.

Father: Our commemoration of Passover is now accomplished. May we celebrate Passover next year in a world at peace, a world of universal freedom.

ALL

Amen!

לַשָּׁנָה הַבָּאָה בִּירוּשָׁלָיִם

Lashana ha-ba-a bi-Y'rushalayim!

Next year in Jerusalem! May the way to Next Year in Jerusalem be open both spiritually and physically to Jews from all lands, particularly where the way has been difficult: to those of the Soviet Union and those in Arab nations, and to the tribes of Beta Yisroael known as the Falasha of Ethiopia, our oldest separated community. May reunion with our people come to all who are estranged, lost, alienated, impeded, anywhere in the world. For all these we pray: Next Year in Jerusalem!

SONGS

Father: It is the custom to linger over the Passover table, with songs and recitations. Here is a riddle, Echad Mi Yodea, for a start:
One, One, who knows what is One?

The recitation proceeds around the table.

FIRST

I know what is One:
One God, of Heaven and Earth.

Father: Two, two, who knows what is two?

SECOND

I know what is two:
Two Tablets of the Law.

ALL

One God, of Heaven and Earth.

Father: Three, three, who knows what is three?

THIRD

I know what is three:
Three father patriarchs.

ALL

Two Tablets of the Law,
One God, of Heaven and Earth.

Father: Four, four, who knows what is four?

FOURTH

I know what is four:
Four mothers in Israel.

ALL

Three father patriarchs,
Two Tablets of the Law,
One God, of Heaven and Earth.

Father: Five, five, who knows what is five?

NEXT

I know what is five:
Five books contain our laws.

ALL

Four mothers in Israel,
Three father patriarchs,
Two Tablets of the Law,
One God, of Heaven and Earth.

Father: Six, six, who knows what is six?

NEXT

I know what is six:
Six books explain our laws.

ALL (*with increasing speed*)

Five books contain our laws,
Four mothers in Israel,
Three father patriarchs,
Two Tablets of the Law,
One God, of Heaven and Earth.

Father: Seven, seven, who knows what is seven?

NEXT

I know what is seven:
Seven days to make a week.

ALL

Six books explain our laws,
Five books contain our laws,
Four mothers in Israel,
Three father patriarchs,
Two Tablets of the Law,
One God, of Heaven and Earth.

Father: Eight, eight, who knows what is eight?

NEXT

I know what is eight:
Eight days before a b'rith.

ALL

Seven days to make a week,
Six books explain our laws,
Five books contain our laws,
Four mothers in Israel,
Three father patriarchs,

Two Tablets of the Law,
One God, of Heaven and Earth.

Father: Nine, nine, who knows what is nine?

NEXT

I know what is nine:
Nine months before a birth.

ALL

Eight days before a b'rith,
Seven days to make a week,
Six books explain our laws,
Five books contain our laws,
Four mothers in Israel,
Three father patriarchs,
Two Tablets of the Law,
One God, of Heaven and Earth.

Father: Ten, ten, who knows what is ten?

NEXT

I know what is ten:
Ten laws in God's command.

ALL

Nine months before a birth,
Eight days before a b'rith,
Seven days to make a week,
Six books explain our laws,
Five books contain our laws,
Four mothers in Israel,
Three father patriarchs,
Two Tablets of the Law,
One God, of Heaven and Earth.

Father: Eleven, eleven, who knows what is eleven?

NEXT

I know what is eleven:
Eleven stars in Joseph's dream.

ALL (*still faster*)

Ten laws in God's command,
Nine months before a birth,
Eight days before a b'rith,
Seven days to make a week,
Six books explain our laws,
Five books contain our laws,
Four mothers in Israel,
Three father patriarchs,
Two Tablets of the Law,
One God, of Heaven and Earth.

Father: Twelve, twelve, who knows what is twelve?

NEXT

I know what is twelve:
Twelve were the tribes in Israel.

ALL (*racing*)

Eleven stars in Joseph's dream,
Ten laws in God's command,
Nine months before a birth,
Eight days before a b'rith,
Seven days to make a week,
Six books explain our laws,
Five books contain our laws,
Four mothers in Israel,
Three father patriarchs,
Two Tablets of the Law,
One God, of Heaven and Earth.

ECHAD MI YODEA

אֶחָד מִי יוֹדֵעַ?
אֶחָד אֲנִי יוֹדֵעַ:
אֶחָד אֱלֹהֵינוּ, שֶׁבַּשָּׁמַיִם וּבָאָרֶץ.

שְׁנַיִם מִי יוֹדֵעַ?
שְׁנַיִם אֲנִי יוֹדֵעַ:
שְׁנֵי לוּחוֹת הַבְּרִית,
אֶחָד אֱלֹהֵינוּ, שֶׁבַּשָּׁמַיִם וּבָאָרֶץ.

Who knows what is One?
I know what is One.
One is the Eternal
Who is in Heaven and on Earth.

Who knows what is two?
I know what is two.
Two Tablets of the Law.
One is the Eternal
Who is in Heaven and on Earth.

CHAD GADYA

One small goat
Chad gadya
Papa bought for two zuzim
One small goat
Chad Gadya! Chad Gadya!

A hungry cat
Ate up the goat
That papa bought for two zuzim
Chad Gadya! Chad Gadya!

Then came a dog
And bit the cat
That ate the goat
That papa bought for two zuzim
Chad Gadya! Chad Gadya!

Then came a stick
And beat the dog
That bit the cat

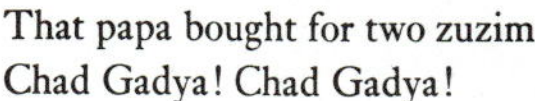

That ate the goat
That papa bought for two zuzim
Chad Gadya! Chad Gadya!

Then came a fire
And burnt the stick
That beat the dog
That bit the cat
That ate the goat
That papa bought for two zuzim
Chad Gadya! Chad Gadya!

Then water came
And quenched the fire
That burnt the stick
That beat the dog
That bit the cat
That ate the goat
That papa bought for two zuzim
Chad Gadya! Chad Gadya!

Then came an ox
And drank the water
That quenched the fire
That burnt the stick
That beat the dog
That bit the cat
That ate the goat
That papa bought for two zuzim
Chad Gadya! Chad Gadya!

The butcher came
And slew the ox
That drank the water
That quenched the fire
That burnt the stick
That beat the dog
That bit the cat
That ate the goat
That papa bought for two zuzim
Chad Gadya! Chad Gadya!

Then came Death
And took the butcher
That slew the ox
That drank the water
That quenched the fire
That burnt the stick
That beat the dog
That bit the cat
That ate the goat
That papa bought for two zuzim
Chad Gadya! Chad Gadya!

Eternity
Dissolves the Death
That took the butcher
That slew the ox
That drank the water
That quenched the fire
That burnt the stick
That beat the dog
That bit the cat
That ate the goat
That papa bought for two zuzim
Chad Gadya! Chad Gadya!
Chad Gad-ya-a-a-a
Chad Gadya!

"Sing out brothers"

HAVA NAGILA

הָבָה נָגִילָה,	Bring on the music And let's have fun!
וְנִשְׂמְחָה.	Start up the dancing too!
הָבָה נְרַנְּנָה,	And let's have fun:
וְנִשְׂמְחָה.	Sing out, sing out brothers, Sing out brothers
עוּרוּ אַחִים	With joy in your hearts Sing out brothers
בְּלֵב שָׂמֵחַ.	With joy in your hearts Sing out, sing out brothers With joy in your hearts!

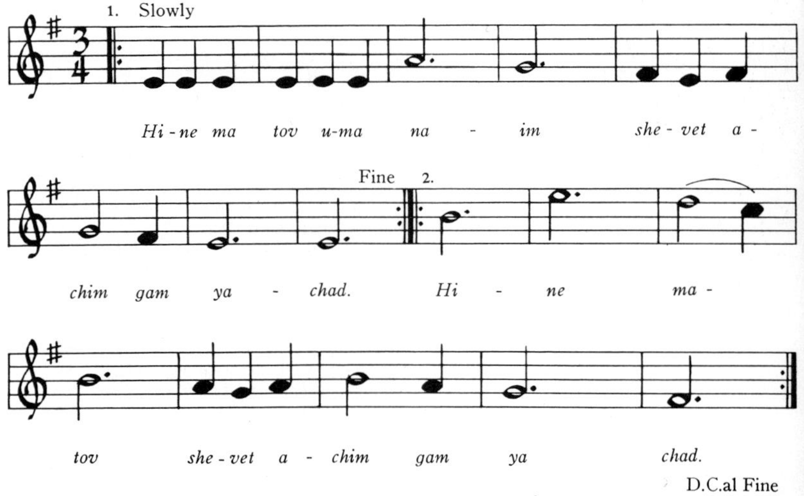

HINE MA TOV!

הִנֵּה מַה טּוֹב וּמַה נָּעִים,
שֶׁבֶת אַחִים גַּם יָחַד.

Here is what's good, nothing's better.
Brothers who dwell together.

A Seder on the beach at Elath near where Moses and the Israelites passed

The hills of Judea

HASHIVENU ELECHA

הֲשִׁיבֵנוּ אֵלֶיךָ וְנָשׁוּבָה,
חַדֵּשׁ יָמֵינוּ כְּקֶדֶם.

Restore us unto Thee and we shall return.
Renew our days as before.

N'RAN'NA

נְרַנְּנָה, נְזַמֵּרָה.	Oh joyously and singingly Oh joyously and singingly
לַ, לַ, לַ . . .	La- la- la! . . .

Hora at Kfar Vitkin

HALLELUYAH

Halleluyah, Halleluyah, Praise Him, Servants of God!
Halleluyah, Halleluyah, Praise ye the name of the Lord!
Halleluyah!
Halleluyah, Halleluyah, for the Name of the Lord shall be Blessed!
Halleluyah, Halleluyah, from this day forevermore!
Halleluyah!

הַלְלוּיָהּ, הַלְלוּיָהּ, הַלְלוּ עַבְדֵי אֲדֹנָי.
הַלְלוּיָהּ, הַלְלוּיָהּ, הַלְלוּ אֶת שֵׁם אֲדֹנָ
הַלְלוּיָהּ.
הַלְלוּיָהּ, הַלְלוּיָהּ, יְהִי שֵׁם אֲדֹנָי מְבֹרָךְ
הַלְלוּיָהּ, הַלְלוּיָהּ, מֵעַתָּה וְעַד עוֹלָם.
הַלְלוּיָהּ.

V'TAHER LIBENU

וְטַהֵר לִבֵּנוּ
לְעָבְדְּךָ בֶּאֱמֶת.

O purify our hearts
O purify our hearts
O purify our hearts
To worship Thee in truth
To worship Thee in truth!

Oasis of Wadi Fara'n, on the way to Mount Sinai

ADIR HU

אַדִּיר הוּא, אַדִּיר הוּא, יִבְנֶה בֵיתוֹ בְּקָרוֹב.
בִּמְהֵרָה, בִּמְהֵרָה, בְּיָמֵנוּ בְּקָרוֹב.
אֵל בְּנֵה, אֵל בְּנֵה, בְּנֵה בֵיתְךָ בְּקָרוֹב.

בָּחוּר הוּא, גָּדוֹל הוּא, יִבְנֶה בֵיתוֹ בְּקָרוֹב.
דָּגוּל הוּא, הָדוּר הוּא, יִבְנֶה בֵיתוֹ בְּקָרוֹב.
וָתִיק הוּא, זַכַּאי הוּא, יִבְנֶה בֵיתוֹ בְּקָרוֹב.
חָסִיד הוּא, טָהוֹר הוּא, יִבְנֶה בֵיתוֹ בְּקָרוֹב.
יָחִיד הוּא, כַּבִּיר הוּא, יִבְנֶה בֵיתוֹ בְּקָרוֹב.

Grand is He, great is He!
He will soon build up His dwelling
And in haste
With all speed
In our time
Very soon
Come and build up
Come and build up
Build Thy dwelling
Very soon!

"Oh joyously and singingly"

BIALIK'S MELODY

HEVENU SHALOM ALEYCHEM

הֵבֵאנוּ שָׁלוֹם עֲלֵיכֶם.

We've brought you
Peace, peace unto you
We've brought you
Peace, peace unto you
We've brought you
Peace, peace unto you
We've brought you
Peace, peace,
Peace, peace,
Peace unto you!

Shalom Aleychem!

PHOTOGRAPH CREDITS

Agor, Ja'acov, Tel Aviv: 79

Baram, Micha (Magnum): 74

Braun, Werner, Jerusalem: 22, 26, 36, 37, 41, 45, 49, 50, 51, 65, 70 right, 71, 93, 99, 100, 113, 118, 121

Cleave, Richard L., Jerusalem: 38 top left, 92

Danin, Avinoam, Jerusalem: 24 top left, 56–57, 66, 81

Ferguson, Walter, Beit Yanai: 38 bottom right

Fusco, Paul (Magnum): 97 bottom

Gaskin, David M., Tel Aviv: 16

Greenwald, Hazel, New York: 7, 15, 16 top, 24–25 bottom, 47, 101, 110, 117, 124

Harbutt, Charles (Magnum): 19

Harris, David, Jerusalem: 27, 29, 35, 40, 75, 76, 77, 91, 123

Kneller, Rolf, Jerusalem: 17, 38 bottom left, 39, 42

Levin, Mikael, Herzlia-on-Sea: 78, 114

Nachtwey, James (Magnum): 97 top

Rosefsky, Steven M., New York: 64, 96

Rothenberg, Dr. Benno, Tel Aviv: 67

Rubinger, David, Jerusalem: 127

Sharpe, Charles, Chicago: 52, 53

Department of Agriculture, Israel: 54